C0-AWW-806

HARVARD THEOLOGICAL STUDIES

HARVARD
THEOLOGICAL STUDIES

EDITED FOR THE

FACULTY OF THEOLOGY

IN

HARVARD UNIVERSITY

BY

GEORGE F. MOORE, JAMES H. ROPES,
KIRSOPP LAKE

CAMBRIDGE
HARVARD UNIVERSITY PRESS
LONDON : HUMPHREY MILFORD
OXFORD UNIVERSITY PRESS
1929

HARVARD THEOLOGICAL STUDIES

XIV

THE SINGULAR PROBLEM OF THE EPISTLE TO THE GALATIANS

BY

JAMES HARDY ROPES

ISSUED AS AN EXTRA NUMBER OF THE
HARVARD THEOLOGICAL REVIEW

CAMBRIDGE
HARVARD UNIVERSITY PRESS
LONDON : HUMPHREY MILFORD
OXFORD UNIVERSITY PRESS
1929

"There's a great text in Galatians,
Once you trip on it, entails
Twenty-nine distinct damnations,
One sure, if another fails."

COPYRIGHT, 1929
BY THE PRESIDENT AND FELLOWS OF
HARVARD COLLEGE

PRINTED AT THE HARVARD UNIVERSITY PRESS
CAMBRIDGE, MASS., U. S. A.

CONTENTS

THE SINGULAR PROBLEM OF THE
EPISTLE TO THE GALATIANS

I

The Problems of the Epistle; W. Lütgert's Theory

THE Epistle of Paul to the Galatians is commonly treated as
if the situation in Galatia which it reflects were entirely clear
and easy to understand. The books on New Testament Introduction speak about that situation with positiveness and confidence, and in the light of the interpretation they all offer it
is customary for historical students to use the epistle freely, not
only for the biography of Paul, but as revealing the partisan
missionary activities of the Jewish believers in Jerusalem at an
early date, and as illuminating the conflict of Jewish Christians
and gentile Christians which is supposed to have continued for
years in Asia Minor and farther west. The chief problems
which recent writers on Galatians have treated as uncertain are
the geographical question of the district intended by 'Galatia,'
the probable place and date at which the epistle was written,
and the relation of the facts mentioned by Paul to the narratives
of the Book of Acts. Within the epistle itself many exegetical
difficulties have presented themselves to commentators and
have defied complete solution, but on the fundamental
question of the nature of the Galatian movement which Paul
is trying to check and the character of the opponents who have
stirred his resentment it has been taken for granted that only
one view is possible. In long discussions of the epistle a few
paragraphs have sufficed for stating, without fear of contradiction, what has seemed to be the whole truth about these central
interests.

This assumption about Galatians has had a direct influence
on the interpretation of the Epistle to the Romans, in which a
situation similar to that in Galatia has commonly been detected
as present at Rome or at least as anticipated there. And inas-

much as many students assign Galatians to an early date in the
period before Paul's arrest and imprisonment, while Romans
certainly comes from a late one, the picture usually drawn of
the whole of that period has been affected, and in some measure
colored, by the accepted view of the Galatian situation. Moreover, from Galatians an interpretation has been imposed upon
the obscure hints which the Epistles to the Corinthians, as well
as that to the Philippians, give of the nature of the controversies
in those cities.

The current view of Galatians may be said to go back probably to Marcion in the second century, to have been exaggerated
by the Tübingen school of the middle of the nineteenth century,
and more lately to have acquired its present moderated form,
as accepted by most recent scholars. Even Lake, who broke
away from the usual representations of the Corinthian epistles
in his "Earlier Epistles of St. Paul" (1911), was content to
treat the Galatian situation itself (apart from questions of geography and date and relation to Acts) in three or four brief
paragraphs.

Ten years ago, however, in 1919 there appeared from an
entirely different point of view a noteworthy investigation of
the Epistle to the Galatians which received too little attention
in the disturbed period immediately following the War and
seems generally to have escaped notice since that time. It came
from Professor Wilhelm Lütgert,[1] then of Halle now of Berlin,
who had previously published a series of studies of epistles of
Paul, and had made an especially interesting and important
contribution to thought on the subject of the Corinthian epistles.[2] Lütgert's contentions, which have given the incentive to

[1] Wilhelm Lütgert, Gesetz und Geist: eine Untersuchung zur Vorgeschichte des
Galaterbriefes (Beiträge zur Förderung christlicher Theologie, XXII. 6), Güters-
loh, 1919. Lütgert's book on Galatians was reviewed by Pott in the Theologische
Literaturzeitung, 1919, cols. 267–268, and by K. Deissner in Die Theologie der
Gegenwart, vol. XIV, 1920, pp. 205–211. Attention is paid to it in the suggestive
but inconclusive paper of A. Fridrichsen, 'Die Apologie des Paulus Gal. 1,' in
L. Brun and A. Fridrichsen, Paulus und die Urgemeinde: zwei Abhandlungen,
Giessen, 1921.

[2] W. Lütgert, Freiheitspredigt und Schwarmgeister in Korinth: ein Beitrag zur
Charakteristik der Christuspartei (Beiträge zur Förderung christlicher Theologie,
XII. 3), 1908.

the present paper, deserve careful consideration. Much of the present essay rests directly on the suggestions and instruction I have received from him, but in presenting what I have to say I have not followed the form of his treatment; and I have not hesitated to use his ideas without giving specific references to the pages of his book. I have not tried to make clear in detail at what points I adhere to him and where I should depart from or add to, his conclusions, but any originality in the conception belongs to Lütgert and not to me. Lütgert also works out very instructively the detailed exegesis of some passages on which I have not found it necessary to dwell for the purposes of this essay.

The general view of Galatians here reached under Lütgert's guidance will be seen to be associated with certain other views regarding the Second Epistle to the Corinthians advocated by Lütgert but held in varying forms by various scholars, notably by Lake. These scholars have brought into prominence elements in the Pauline churches not allowed for in the Tübingen formula nor adequately estimated in the picture of the scene to which that formula was presently forced to yield place.

The essence of the matter in the Epistle to the Galatians is that there are, as all admit, two elements in the Galatian situation, first, the judaizing tendency which Paul reproves, and secondly, the hostile personal attacks upon Paul which he endeavors to repel. The usual view explains the attacks referred to by Paul as proceeding from the judaizers; Lütgert's view explains them as made not by the judaizers but by a 'radical' party in the Galatian churches which stood in opposition both to the judaizers and to Paul.

In what follows I shall first bring forward the difficulties which on various sides attach to the commonly held, and simple, theory of the situation. I will then try to state clearly the alternative, and somewhat more complicated, theory which is here proposed. Finally, in a brief running commentary on the six successive chapters of the epistle I shall seek to apply this proposed theory to Paul's course of thought, and thus to show that it well explains the whole epistle, and is free from the difficulties of the usual theory.

II

Difficulties in the Usual Interpretation of 3, 1–5, 10

First, grave difficulties attend the usual theory even in the half of the epistle on which that theory is chiefly founded.

The main positive affirmation of the epistle is perfectly clear, and disagreement with regard to it can hardly arise. About one-half of the letter, the section beginning with 3, 1 and running through 5, 6 (or rather, going as far as 5, 10) is occupied with exposition and appeal largely intended to convince the readers that for a believer in Jesus Christ to submit himself to the Jewish Law and allow himself to be circumcised is nothing short of complete apostasy from Christ. It is evident that in the churches of Galatia there was actually a movement in that direction, and at the close of the epistle (6, 12–13) Paul impatiently declares that the promoters of it (apparently, according to this passage, themselves Christian believers) are actuated by selfish and cowardly motives. In the mind of those affected by the movement, as we gather from the whole course of the epistle, this inclination did not contemplate a withdrawal from Christian fellowship, but rather an additional security for their salvation; it was a kind of system of 're-insurance.'

In urging that such action as was proposed would be unreasonable, unnecessary, and disastrous, Paul appeals to the fact that faith in Christ, by itself and without reinforcement through works of the Law, has by the gift of the Spirit consequent upon it been manifestly attested to possess the favor of God (3, 2–5); and he declares (3, 10–12; 3, 21) that the Law imposes a curse and cannot lead to salvation. The salvation for which we hope rests on our faith in Christ, and our inheritance of salvation is assured to us by the Spirit (3, 13–14; 4, 6; 5, 5). Paul's precise view of the Law is carefully made plain in an elaborate discussion (3, 15–25). It was, indeed, given by God, but subsequently to the promise to Abraham; it had a strictly limited function and, in particular, was of only temporary validity. By the death of Christ, the Son of God, whom, it is emphasized, God sent into the world not only as a man but as a Jew (4, 4), the Law lost its binding force. Anyone, Greek or Jew, bond or free, male or female, who by faith unites himself with Christ, is a son of Abraham, entitled to a share in the promises made to Abraham (3, 26–29), which the later promulgation of the temporary Law did not, and could not, disannul (3, 17). On the other hand, the relation between Christian believers and unbelieving Jews is expounded by the allegorical use of Old Testament history (4, 21–31). We Christians, it is here explained, are Abraham's children by the freewoman, his wife; the Jews represent only the inferior line of descent from the bondwoman Hagar. A permanent separation and even hostility subsists between the two (4, 29–30); the Jews have in fact persecuted the Christians, while the Christian church is directed by Scripture (Gen. 21, 10) to separate itself from unbelieving Jews.

This whole portion of the epistle, from chapter 3 to a point early in chapter 5, deals with a single large topic, and there can be no doubt as to the author's main drift. The only questionable part is the section 4, 12–20, where the author turns to a kind of personal appeal, containing many obscure allusions to facts unknown to us but nowhere leading to any different view of the general context in which it stands. Paul sets forth his thought at large and with such fullness as to reveal his position clearly, and thus the main feature of the situation in Galatia which evokes the argument is made plain. Christians in these churches are in danger of accepting Judaism, and so, to put the matter in our own language, of reducing Christianity to the position of a Jewish sect, tolerated by the Jews because of the faithful observance which Christians would then render to the Jewish Law, but from Paul's point of view subject to the reproach of having denied Christ and abandoned divine grace.

But although all this is clear and indisputable, yet, even in this portion of the epistle there remains on a closer inspection something to be explained which is not covered by the account of the situation just given. Paul's argument against the gentile Christians who wish to add the Law to their faith, closely resembling as it does in some respects certain passages of the

Epistle to the Romans, is, indeed, enunciated with the utmost decisiveness. He abhors the proposal, and shrinks from no sharpness or directness of statement. In compact form he presents positive and convincing declarations (3, 1–5; 3, 10–12; 3, 21; 4, 9; 5, 1–4) of the futility of the Law as a means of salvation, and intersperses vigorous affirmations of the saving work of Christ and the efficacy of faith in Him. His aim is sure, and his shafts hit the mark. Nevertheless, in the part beginning with 3, 6, his argument is founded on the assumption that Christian faith is not devoid of a positive relation to the Hebrew tradition and even to the Law, and it is noticeable what pains he takes to affirm and define this positive relation. For some reason he feels it important to show that his rejection of the Law as a ground of salvation is not inconsistent with a firm belief in the importance of the Hebrew tradition for Christians. The promises to Abraham are treated as fundamental in God's saving work; the Law, though strictly temporary, yet had had its definite part to play; Christ came into the world as a Jew (4, 4); it is by the Law itself (4, 21), in the story of Abraham's two sons, that the opposition between unbelieving Jews and believers in Christ is stated and that the present opportunity of entering upon freedom in place of slavery is prophetically announced. Even the repeated statement that there is no dividing line in Christ between circumcised and uncircumcised believers (3, 28; 5, 6; and again, at the close, in 6, 15) may be taken as the express repudiation of a possible suggestion that gentile Christians alone are true believers. Paul keeps telling his readers that faith makes them all sons of Abraham (3, 7; 3, 9; 3, 14; 3, 29). This prominence given to the positive relation to Israel of Christian believers recalls, in spite of differences between the two passages, the warning allegory of the 11th chapter of Romans. In both passages Paul impresses upon the gentile Christians that they have been introduced from outside into the Hebrew tradition, and in both passages this is represented as a privilege. So also in Romans 4 the direct relation of Christian believers to Abraham and to his faith is elaborately explained.

Now all this side of Paul's argument creates a difficulty. Such a statement as 3, 7, "Know therefore that they which be of faith, the same are sons of Abraham," would seem to rest on the assumption that to 'sons of Abraham' alone belongs salvation. This was the conviction of the Jews, and, in his own sense, it was the conviction of Paul; but the persons whom Paul is here trying to convince are not Jews but gentiles, and as such can have no original interest in Abraham, deeply as they are interested in salvation. The Jews would have offered them salvation through circumcision and consequent incorporation into the Jewish nation and religion; and such proselytes would have a comprehensible interest in being sons of Abraham. Paul, on the other hand, in order to preclude any such act, urges on these gentiles the doctrine that circumcision has no saving efficacy. From the gentile point of view (as distinct from Paul's own) that would seem to settle the matter, and to leave no place for the requirement of sonship to Abraham, any more than for that of the circumcision which in the natural order of things effects such sonship. Why, then, after having made his point with perfect definiteness (3, 2–5), does Paul himself drag in sonship to Abraham, and go on to explain that for becoming sons of Abraham the method of faith is as good a method as that of circumcision, indeed a better one than circumcision? Surely, if a gentile had not been actually converted to Judaism, the comment he would make on being told that gentiles by exercising faith in Christ become sons of Abraham would be, 'Why should I be interested in becoming a son of Abraham?' What Paul's readers crave is not sonship to Abraham for its own sake, but salvation; and that, as Paul tells them, comes solely through faith in Christ. Why this roundabout method of further argument?

If we are to suppose that Paul is here guided purely by the purpose of his controversy against judaizing tendencies, it must be admitted that at this juncture he makes a concession, the concession, namely, that sonship to Abraham is needed in order to obtain a right to the promises of God. By conceding this he is brought under the necessity of elaborately setting forth sub-

tleties not easily comprehensible at a first reading then or now
(3, 13–18). And he is further led to expound carefully and at
some length the precise and very delicately balanced view in
which he combines respect for the Law with the complete rejection of it (3, 19–29). These ideas are undoubtedly highly important to Paul himself in his own thinking, but in this critical
issue, where Christian gentiles are on the verge of a conversion
(even though only a supplementary one) to Judaism, they clog
Paul's counter-argument, and the introduction of them seems
to constitute at least a qualified admission, and a dangerous
one, of some degree of plausibility in the contentions of those
who seek to pervert the Galatians.

The problem which confronts us in trying fully to understand
Paul's discussion in these chapters is more serious than is often
perceived. The solution usually given is that Paul chooses his
position in order to meet the arguments brought by Jewish
Christians who are working on the minds of gentile believers.
With that explanation we have to assume that these gentiles
have been indoctrinated (either by these present Jewish Christian emissaries or by previous contact with the synagogue) with
the idea that everything turns on the promises to Abraham and
that to be a 'son of Abraham' is essential for their salvation,
but that they have not yet yielded to the emissaries' urgent
demand that they submit to circumcision in order to become
'sons of Abraham.' Just at this point Paul will be understood
to enter the discussion. He will be regarded as explaining that
if you deem it necessary to become a 'son of Abraham,' a better
path to that goal than circumcision is faith in Christ.

The assumption of this peculiar situation, definitely limited
on the one side as to the precise extent to which the Galatian
Christians have already yielded to the emissaries' arguments
and on the other by their refusal as yet to go beyond that
point, can hardly be escaped, if the usual solution, stated above,
is adopted. Against such a view, however, there are two objections. First, in verse 6 Paul introduces the discussion of Abraham not at all as if it were the premise of his opponents, with
which he has to reckon in the controversy, but quite as his own

idea, brought in by reason of his own interests in order to illustrate the general view which he himself wishes to make clear. So also in the following verses it presently appears that the reference to Abraham is more than a passing illustration; it is an integral element in his own system of thought. Secondly, even if this objection be disregarded, the conception which the usual solution requires is not at all easy to picture, and is too narrow. This has perhaps been made sufficiently clear by what has been said above. The solution commonly proposed cannot, therefore, be regarded as satisfactory, although perhaps it cannot be called impossible.

In view of these difficulties a different solution commends itself, and may by anticipation be briefly outlined. Since verse 7 does not introduce a second argument strictly parallel to Paul's highly effective appeal to the facts, and since for attaining Paul's primary purpose the passage would have been stronger if he had left out the greater part of what follows, may it not be that this whole discussion of Abraham and of the proper function of the Law is introduced here for some reason extraneous to the immediate argument against the judaizers? This section of the epistle offers two contentions: (1) faith in Christ is the only way of salvation, and a gentile believer must not subject himself to the Jewish Law but between Christian believers and unbelieving Jews there must be permanent opposition; (2) the Law was once valid but has now lapsed, and the believer in Christ, though a gentile, is in full reality brought by faith into direct relation to Abraham and to the promises made to Abraham. The former of these two contentions reveals to us the situation in Galatia. The latter of them presents Paul's general view, otherwise in part at least known to us, of the positive relation of Christians to the promises to Israel, and his theory of the positive significance of the Law in God's work of salvation; but, as has been argued above, Paul's extended treatment here of this latter subject is not adequately accounted for by the situation which we infer from the first contention. If we could believe that in the whole section he is not merely opposing the judaizing tendency, but is at the same time defending his own position against attack from a different quarter and urging that his belief in the enduring significance of the Hebrew tradition (compare Rom. 4 and 9–11) is fully consistent with recognition of the absolute efficacy of faith in Christ, both aspects of the passage would be explained.

The possibility of such an explanation of the passage is suggested by the view, convincingly presented by recent studies of the Corinthian epistles, that in the gentile world Paul's most dangerous opponents were not judaizers, as at Antioch and Jerusalem, but radicals of the opposite stripe. These latter persons tended to cut off Christianity altogether from its roots in the Jewish religion, to insist upon the completely new status into which the gift of the Holy Spirit introduces believers, to emphasize their own supernatural 'knowledge,' and to think of themselves as so completely possessed by the Spirit of God that, living 'according to the Spirit,' they were exempt from concern for the things of the flesh, even from those distinctions of right and wrong and from that moral discipline which were a fundamental interest in Paul's mind. In a word, these people were spiritual 'perfectionists,' who, although at least in some cases Jews by birth, eagerly grasped the revolutionary side of Paul's teaching and carried it to a logical extreme which resulted in a sharp clash with the apostle. For want of a better name we may call them 'pneumatici,' 'spiritual persons,' as Paul seems to do in various passages, or 'radicals.' Their activity is most prominently reflected in the Corinthian epistles, but the same general tendency would naturally present itself elsewhere, and it seems to have caused Paul much anxiety. The development in the second century of Gnostic doctrine and Marcion's schism shows that his concern was justified.[3]

If the existence of this type of opponents of Paul in the gentile churches be admitted and this tendency borne in mind in the study of the Epistle to the Galatians, the chief difficulties of the

---

[3] On this view of the Corinthian epistles see Lütgert, Freiheitspredigt und Schwarmgeister in Korinth, 1908; K. Lake, The Earlier Epistles of St. Paul, 1911; and the volumes in Meyer's Kommentar by Johannes Weiss on 1 Corinthians (1910) and by H. Windisch on 2 Corinthians (1924).

epistle disappear, or are greatly diminished, including many of those which must frequently have left the interpreter (as he has certainly left his readers) with a disquieting sense of something perfunctory and unilluminating in his results.[4] The application to Galatians in more detail will be attempted at a later point in this essay.

[4] Holtzmann (Einleitung in das Neue Testament, 3rd ed., 1892, p. 219) observes that "Galatians, on its face one of the most transparent pieces of writing in the New Testament, may well be counted among the more difficult New Testament problems."

III

The Charges against Paul (1, 1–2, 21; 5, 11–6, 18)

Observing, then, that from Galatians 3, 1—5, 10 we obtain a satisfactory knowledge of Paul's own teaching, but are left in some doubt as to whether the judaizing movement suffices to account for all the elements of the situation in Galatia, we next turn to the other half of the epistle, far more varied in content, of which one section (1, 1—2, 21) precedes, and the other (5, 11—6, 18) follows, the half we have been examining.

These passages now to be considered are unlike 3, 1—5, 10, in that we get from them what we do not gain from those chapters, namely, repeated and abundant evidence of some kind of personal attack upon Paul which he bitterly resents and to which he here replies in a good deal of heat. Whereas 3, 1—5, 10 to a certain extent resembles Romans, in this other half of Galatians some parts recall the temper and manner of Second Corinthians.[5] In much of what he says here Paul seems to be on the defensive, not of his own accord striking out to repress Galatian error.

We must first inquire what Paul says, or fairly implies, as to the opposition which has attacked him. Doubtful passages should be postponed until a later point.

The opening section of the letter (1, 1—2, 14; the following verses, 2, 15–21, being of disputable meaning and application) is largely occupied with claims by Paul for himself personally and for his gospel, apparently in reply to hostile statements or insinuations made against him in Galatia from a source the nature of which is nowhere definitely stated. From this whole passage, with which 5, 11 is to be associated, the following points can be definitely elicited. Most of them are obvious and well known.

---

[5] An effective statement of the similarity between Galatians and Second Corinthians, partly quoted from Jowett, is to be found in Lightfoot's commentary (pp. 44 f.). Lightfoot also gives (pp. 45–48) a full table of parallels with Romans.

(1) Paul says that he is an Apostle commissioned directly by God without even so much as intermediation from man (1, 1):

Paul, Apostle, not from men nor through a man but through Jesus Christ and God the Father who raised him from the dead.

We need not infer from his language that his apostleship had been expressly denied, but it seems clear that someone had affirmed that it came to him "through a man" and that he therefore lacked independent divine authority for his teaching. At least, in the attack made on his authority he must have been practically treated *as if* he had had no divine commission.

This inference as to the attack is supported by the elaborate statements in 1, 13—2, 14, where an explanation is given of Paul's relation to the Jerusalem apostles. The charge which he repels in both passages seems to have been that he had been dependent for his gospel on some one or more of these apostles.

(2) Paul declares with great intensity that his gospel is the same now that it has always been (1,8–10):

But even if we, or an angel from heaven, preach the gospel to you in departure from what we preached to you, let him be anathema. As we have said before, now again I say, if anyone is preaching the gospel to you in departure from what you received, let him be anathema. For am I now striving for the favor of men or of God? or am I seeking to please men? If I were still pleasing men, I should not be Christ's servant.

His gospel has not been altered or adjusted in order to win the favor of men by insincerely echoing or in any manner conforming to their views. What the Galatians received from him in the beginning was his sincere and complete and unchangeable gospel, and he preaches nothing other at the present time.

All this implies unmistakably that he has been accused of time-serving and changing his tone, but in what direction — whether that of a fuller recognition of the importance of the Hebrew tradition for Christians or that of a more drastic severance of Christian faith from Jewish customs and principles — is not clearly indicated. Even the word "still" (vs. 10) does not make this point clear. (The word probably has the sense of 'as before my conversion to Christ'; the purpose of the sentence is to repudiate a calumny brought against Paul, he makes no admission that at any time the charge would have been well founded.)

(3) From his own conduct Paul then turns to his gospel, and affirms that he did not get it from any man but that it was revealed to him by God (1, 11–12):

> For I make known to you, brethren, the gospel preached by me, th. t it is not according to man; for not from a man did I receive it, nor was I taught it, but through Jesus Christ's revelation.

In this statement he seems to be directly repelling the disparaging fling of his opponents that his is a human gospel.

(4) By the succeeding statement of facts from his life Paul substantiates the divine origin of his gospel (1, 15–16) and his independence of any direct influence from the Jerusalem apostles at any period. To this we must return later. For our immediate purpose it is enough to repeat that a part of the attack upon him is here plainly shown to have consisted in the charge that he has been dependent for his gospel on Jewish believers in Judaea. The incident at Antioch (2, 11–14) is introduced to show that he has even been aggressive in maintaining his independent attitude.

The narrative finally merges in a statement of his religious position (2, 15–21). The interpretation of this highly important and difficult passage will turn on the interpreter's view as to where the emphasis in the balanced sentences is intended to fall; since its bearing is questionable, it cannot be used here.

(5) Herewith is concluded the first division of the letter. In it Paul is mainly on the defensive, and hence what he says reveals the nature of the attacks that he is rebutting. Of the next division (3, 1—5, 10) the main purpose is attack, not defense, and it does not directly furnish information about the charges against Paul, although the fact of personal hostility to Paul in Galatia is referred to sharply in 4, 16–17:

> So then have I become your enemy by dealing truthfully with you? They are not honorably zealous for you but wish to shut you out in order that you may be zealous for them.

In 5, 11, however, we find a direct reference to his enemies, and, after the discussion of 3, 1—5, 10 just preceding, it is a surprising one. "If," says Paul, "I am still preaching circumcision, why am I still persecuted?" There can be but one inference from this, namely, that some opponents have accused Paul of "still preaching circumcision." Here again, as in 1, 10 (upon which light is thrown by 5, 11), the word 'still' is probably a reference to the days before Paul's conversion, but, even so, in the light of 5, 3–4 we should not have expected any such temerity from any quarter, however hostile.

For our present purpose the ethical section (5, 13—6, 10) cannot be used, for the author's probable motive in introducing it is disputed.

In Galatians, then, it is clear that besides sharply reproving the tendency to adopt Jewish rites (3, 1—5, 10; 6, 12-13) Paul is repelling charges against himself:

(a) of having received his gospel at the hand of man, so that he lacks the authority of a divinely commissioned apostle;
(b) of having dishonorably tried to please men;
(c) of having been dependent on the Jerusalem apostles;
(d) of still preaching circumcision.

So far as I can see, these four points, although forming a summary considerably more meagre than the account of the subject given in many modern discussions, include everything that Paul's defense directly and unambiguously implies as to the charges of those who have attacked him.

IV

The Current Theory of the Situation in Galatia, and its Difficulties

The almost universal practice of students of the Epistle to the Galatians has taken the charges against Paul as made from the side of the judaizing movement in Galatia. This usual theory is based on Gal. 3, 1–5, 10, combined with the narrative of Acts 15. It may be briefly stated as follows:

After the foundation of Paul's gentile churches in Galatia the extreme judaizing party from Judaea, who in Antioch (Acts 15, 1) had told the gentile Christians that to be saved they must become circumcised and at Jerusalem had continued their controversy with Paul and Barnabas, sent a mission to Galatia, and there presented to the gentile Christians the same necessary condition of salvation in direct opposition to Paul's well-known teaching of freedom from the Law. (Whether this effort of propaganda was supported by any of the Twelve Apostles, or by James, has been a matter of dispute among scholars.) In order to make their impression on the Galatian gentile Christians these emissaries reinforced their contradiction of Paul's doctrine by seeking to undermine his influence through bitter attacks against his person and character. He was, they said, no real Apostle, with a divine commission like that of the Twelve, but was, and had repeatedly shown himself, dependent on them. Moreover he was a time-server, and elsewhere than in Galatia and on other occasions than the present had tried to win the favor of men by actually preaching circumcision. As for his doctrine of salvation by faith in Christ without circumcision and the Law, the emissaries, while not denying that Jesus is the Messiah, insisted that the way to salvation is through the Law, and perhaps further urged (although scholars have not been unanimous in inferring this from Paul's words in Gal. 5, 13—6, 10) that Paul's doctrine of free salvation was sure to lead to an intolerable moral laxity. Altogether he was an untrustworthy leader, whose particular teaching, although

he had founded the churches in Galatia, was not entitled longer
to carry weight.

This view of the situation brings under a single conception
both the elements of the epistle. Once accepted, it can be
further elaborated, and the picture enriched, from many hints
in the epistle which are in themselves ambiguous and to which
I have so far not adverted. It has been presented (with various
differences in detail) by nearly all the books on the subject and
was substantially that of the ancient commentators — Chrysostom,[6] Theodore of Mopsuestia, Jerome, Ambrosiaster. Something much like it seems to be stated in the neat second-century
prologue commonly attributed to a Marcionite origin:

> Galatae sunt Graeci. Hi verbum veritatis primum ab
> apostolo acceperunt sed post discessum ejus temptati sunt
> a falsis apostolis ut in legem et circumcisionem verterentur.
> Hos apostolus revocat ad fidem veritatis, scribens eis ab
> Epheso.

Now if the only important controversy on any large matter
in the period occupied by Paul's missionary activity had been
the controversy between Paul and the judaizers (as described
in Acts 15), if, as Lightfoot says (Commentary, p. 311), "hence-
forth [that is, after the Jerusalem conference of Acts 15] St.
Paul's career was one life-long conflict with Judaizing antago-
nists," this theory would be almost unavoidable, and would
have to be applied, as well as might be, to everything in the
epistle. But in the light of the recent views already mentioned about the opponents of Paul in Corinth and perhaps
elsewhere, another possible theory presents itself, and certain
difficulties under the prevalent theory, which have often been
recognized as somewhat disquieting, become more pressing and
less easy to put up with as permanent obscurities due to our
ignorance. In a word, we have to ask whether, after all, the
bitter assailants in Galatia were surely judaizers or whether
they may have been spiritualist radicals ('pneumatici'), like
those whom many scholars believe to have made trouble in

---

[6] Chrysostom, Homilies on Acts xxxvii. 2 (on Acts 17, 2; ed. Montfaucon),
says: καὶ αἱ ἐπιστολαὶ δι' αὐτοῦ πρὸς Ἰουδαίους πᾶσαί εἰσιν ἀπομαχόμεναι.

Corinth.[7] It may be said at once that each theory leaves some facts imperfectly accounted for, but this latter one seems to have at least an equal claim with the former on our candid consideration. Before trying to apply it to the facts we must look at the difficulties under which the prevalent theory labors.

The first passage to be considered will be the opening section (1, 1—2, 14), together with the related passage, 5, 11. The autobiographical argument of 1, 13—2, 14 must here be our main guide. Since the problem of the central section (3, 1—5, 10) has already been discussed, we can then pass on to the ethical section, 5, 13—6, 10.

At the outset, and before proceeding to the positive difficulties, it is to be observed that the opening section (1, 1—2, 14), taken by itself and apart from the later chapters of the epistle, is far less definite in its implications than is often supposed. In the whole passage the only indications that would naturally lead us (and that only indirectly) to infer a judaizing movement in Galatia at all are to be found in the reference to Titus (2, 3–5) and possibly in that to the "false brethren" at Jerusalem "who, in order to enslave you, had smuggled themselves in to spy out our freedom which we have by virtue of our relation to Christ" (2, 4), for the strong emphasis here on Paul's resistance to judaizers at Jerusalem suggests that a similar issue has now arisen in Galatia. What we do learn with certainty is that in Galatia Paul has been declared to lack a divine commission and to have been dependent on the Jerusalem apostles. With

---

[7] De Wette, in his commentary on Galatians (Kurzgefasstes exegetisches Handbuch zum Neuen Testament, 2nd ed., 1845, pp. 74 f., on Gal. 5, 1–13) seems to have had, as Lütgert points out, an inkling of this possibility, at least for the ethical section of Galatians. He wrote: "Es scheint, dass bei den Galatern die freiern paulinischen Christen und die zum Judenthume sich hinneigenden mit einander in Streit lagen, und dass die erstern dabei die hoffärtigen spielten. Diese warnt nun P. vor dem Misbrauche der Freiheit zur Befriedigung ihres Stolzes, und ermahnt sie zur Liebe; dabei erinnert er sowohl sie als die Andern daran, dass das Princip des Gesetzes selbst (um das sich der Streit drehete) die Liebe sei." Perhaps in consequence of this sentence of De Wette, Lightfoot (on 5, 13, Commentary, 10th ed., p. 208) admits, "It may be that here, as in the Corinthian Church, a party opposed to the Judaizers had shown a tendency to Antinomian excess," and again (on 6, 1, p. 215), in rejecting such a view, carefully guards his language: "The epistle however betrays no very distinct traces of the existence of such a party in the Galatian Churches."

much circumstantiality and spirit he denies both these deroga-
tory statements; but from what quarter these reproaches have
proceeded is not made clear to us. Any opponent of his teaching
would naturally have denied his divine commission, and, as has
been pointed out above, judaizers are not the only enemies who
were capable of presenting his relation to Jerusalem in an un-
favorable light. On the face of Paul's language it is by no means
certain whether in 2, 1–10 he advances the fortunate result of
his conference with the leading men at Jerusalem with pride as
a victory, or whether, while he admits the conference to be a
fact, his interest lies in defending his conduct as having been
harmless to his independence. Is he saying, 'The Jerusalem
apostles actually went so far as to give me recognition' or is he
saying, 'All that the Jerusalem apostles did was to give me recognition'? On the former assumption, the charge to which he
replies would be attributed to the judaizers; on the latter, to
the radicals.

For the ordinary theory of the situation in Galatia, the following considerations seem to me embarrassing.
1. In chapter 2 it is clear that the controversy has somehow
turned on Paul's relation to the Jerusalem apostles, which he
so elaborately explains. The usual view is that his judaizing
opponents had appealed against Paul to the authority of these
apostles, and that it is in reply to this that Paul affirms his
independent divine commission and tells how he forced these
authorities to recognize the testimony borne to him by God's
manifest favor. Lightfoot (pp. 27 f.) thus states the position
of Paul's opponents: "It was therefore to the mother Church
of Jerusalem that all questions must be referred, to the great
Apostles of the Circumcision especially, the 'pillars of the
Church,' to James . . . to Peter . . . to John," and again (p. 28,
note 1) he speaks of "the exclusive importance which the Judaizers in Galatia attached to the Apostles of the Circumcision."
But the value of such an appeal by the judaizers would
depend on whether in fact the Jerusalem apostles actually
did give their support to the judaizers' contention that gentile
Christians must subject themselves to the Jewish Law, and

Paul states in his reply (Gal. 2, 6–9) that these authorities had refused to support this contention, while the Book of Acts gives exactly the same representation, both directly in Acts 15 and by implication in Acts 21, 19–20 ("And they [i.e. James and the elders at Jerusalem], when they heard it, glorified God"; note that vs. 18 seems to show that this is a part of the 'we-section'). Therefore, on the current theory we have to assume that the judaizers misrepresented their own authorities; and although, owing to the modern reader's natural and justified inclination to take Paul's side, this idea does not offend him, yet the situation remains a remarkable one, and the temerity, as well as mendacity, of the judaizers would be surprising enough to raise some question as to the theory which requires us to assume it. The facts which Paul states must have been a matter of common knowledge. By simply recounting them he is able to deal a crushing blow to the supposed appeal of the judaizers to the Jerusalem apostles; he has merely to remind them that these apostles had given to him, not to the judaizing faction, their support on this critical occasion. So fatuous an appeal would certainly be extraordinary. It may be recalled that these verses of Galatians constitute one of the chief rocks on which the Tübingen construction was finally wrecked.

2. But even if we disregard the difficulty just discussed about the judaizers' relation to Jerusalem, and suppose it possible that the judaizers honestly believed themselves to be in general harmony with the Jewish believers of Jerusalem and their apostolic leaders (though doubtless in perfect agreement with only the radical element in that church), what do we find on the current theory? The judaizers are of course supposed to attack Paul primarily because he preaches freedom from the Law. That is the gravamen of their objection to him, and their own fidelity to the Law is their great link of connection with the Jerusalem church. But they have complained of Paul that his gospel was received from man and is according to man, and Paul's mode of answering, by showing, as he does, how little contact since his conversion he has had with the believers and apostles *at Jerusalem*, and by explaining the nature of that contact, makes it clear that the alleged human source, or media-

tion, of his gospel was located at Jerusalem among these specific brethren. Consequently, by the current theory the judaizers are represented as trying to undermine Paul's work by declaring that he had accepted authority and received influence from the very group with which they themselves had substantial sympathy. Dependence on such authorities, it would seem, ought rather to have been a merit in their eyes than a source of discredit.

To save the current theory from this paradoxical representation of the facts it is possible to dissociate the two grounds of attack (the one that of inferior rank, the other of subjection to Jerusalem), and to regard the contemptuous allegation of Paul's inferior rank as standing, as it were, quite by itself, made with complete indifference to the question of who the authorities were to whom he was inferior. But the difficulty of so unnatural a distinction is obvious, and the method of Paul's reply, with its pointed references to the Jerusalem apostles and the Judaean churches, and to these alone, is at variance with any such idea. The infelicity of a general theory which requires such an unlikely supposition can hardly be denied; [8] and the destructive force of the whole curious paradox can be neglected only in case no other defensible theory of the situation can be proposed.

3. Another difficulty for the current theory in this passage has to do with the charge of "seeking to please men" (1, 10). General abuse of Paul on the ground of his personal character and supposed vacillation of purpose is known to us from other epistles (for instance, 1 Thess. 2, 3; 2 Cor. 1, 15–17), and of course might be the expression of any type of hostility to him. But in Galatians, as we have seen, the accusation of self-seeking compliance (1, 10) is supplemented, and probably explained, by the charge, to which he makes explicit reply in 5, 11, of "preaching circumcision." Now this is a most extraordinary charge for judaizers to bring, whose own chief business at the moment was itself to "preach circumcision." We could understand such an allegation by them if they had claimed Paul as an ally, but Paul here evidently treats the statement as a hostile

[8] This point is effectively brought out in Fridrichsen's paper mentioned above.

charge, to be repudiated with indignation, and his manner makes it probable that the matter was considered important. So far as the charge itself is concerned, it is not difficult to believe that Paul had indeed so spoken and acted as to give it color; in that case he would all the more have resented it. The difficulty lies in supposing that those from whom the fling came were judaizers. The usual mode of escape is by saying, as in the case of the charge of inferiority, that not the direction, but the mere fact, of Paul's supposed vacillation was what the judaizers complained of, and that the trait signalized would have been in any case discreditable. This is, again, an answer to the difficulty, but not one that leaves the questioner satisfied.

And even apart from the indications of 5, 11, Paul's mode of refuting in chapters 1 and 2 the allegation of changes in his gospel by way of conformity (1, 8–10), if the judaizers are supposed to have made it, creates the same puzzling problem as in the case of the charge of his dependence on men. It would be very hard to believe that the judaizers had complained of Paul for occasionally conforming to their own special ideas. Surely what they objected to must have been acts on his part looking in the *opposite* direction. Yet when he presently comes to his full reply (and verses 11–12 cannot be isolated either from verses 8–10 or from verse 13), he makes it, and that with the greatest insistence (note the asseveration with a kind of oath in 1, 20), by demonstrating from the actual facts how slight has been his contact not with persons who might have seemed to the judaizers likely to exert a bad influence on him and lead him astray, but with the judaizers' own friends at Jerusalem.

4. One other burden under which the current theory labors is to be observed in a different part of the epistle. With 5, 13 the apostle turns to a considerable section of ethical exhortation (5, 13—6, 10) which opens with a warning against allowing the liberty which he preaches to degenerate into license. Of course pastoral advice on morals may be deemed always needed, but that does not well account for what seem the specific allusions of this section, nor is mere general advice to be expected in this epistle, with its manifest definiteness of purpose. Moreover, the

section is by its nature a qualification, not a reinforcement, of Paul's affirmation of complete Christian freedom. Hence many scholars have treated the section as the reply to a supposed objection by the judaizers that Paul's doctrine of freedom from the Law opens the way to moral laxity. He, they say, here takes the opportunity to show what his moral demands really are, and so to make it impossible to complain that they are not strict. But of any such purpose the passage gives no sign. It sounds like a straightforward warning against lax tendencies, addressed to persons who really needed it; it does not sound like an exhibition, for the purposes of argument, of the way in which Paul *would be* capable of treating the matter if he were actually writing to readers who did need the warning. The failure of the current theory to explain well this ethical section is not fatal, but it is a distinct weakness in the theory.

We have already seen in the earlier part of this essay that even Paul's direct rebuke, in the section 3, 1—5, 10, of voluntary submission to the Jewish Law is not well accounted for in every particular merely by the judaizing movement which he is ostensibly reproving. His argument in those chapters is burdened by lengthy discussions in which a relation of gentile Christians to Abraham and to the covenant with Abraham is assumed and accepted, the positive (although temporary) value of the Law emphasized, and the birth of Jesus Christ as a Jew, under the Law, made prominent — and all this with no hint of making a mere concession, but seemingly as an integral element in Paul's own thought. To this indication that the Galatian situation was less simple than is usually supposed can now be added, by way of summary of what has been discussed above, the following points in which the usual theory of the situation does not adequately explain the other sections (1, 1—2, 21 and 5, 11—6, 18):

(1) The supposed appeal of the judaizers to the Jerusalem apostles is odd, since precisely the main contention of the judaizers was not shared by the Jerusalem apostles.

(2) The combination of the judaizers' rejection of Paul's gospel of freedom with the coincident charge by them that he

had learned his gospel from their own friends produces a paradox.

(3) That he preaches circumcision is a singular ground for an attack on him by those who also preach it; and even if the charge of unworthy motives in veering with the wind of human favor be taken to refer not to this but to his turning away from the truth as taught at Jerusalem in order to adopt his doctrine of freedom, certainly his method of countering that charge, by showing that he has been independent of Jerusalem, is a strange one.

(4) Extensive ethical instruction is introduced (5, 13—6, 10) which, if merely pastoral, is hardly in place in this letter and distinctly weakens Paul's main contention in behalf of freedom, while, if it is a rebuttal directed against the judaizers' misrepresentations, it is strangely devoid of any indication whatever of its purpose.

As has been said already, the use of the book for an understanding of Paul's own religious ideas does not depend on any theory of the Galatian situation and of the attack on Paul; nevertheless many parts of the epistle cannot be satisfactorily interpreted without such a theory, and the current theory is so loaded with difficulties that it is hard to accept it, unless it is the only possible theory. If no other theory could be proposed, we should probably have to overlook the difficulties of the current one and take refuge in our own insuperable ignorance of the real circumstances.

An alternative theory can, however, be suggested. Its acceptability depends on whether it suits the facts of the epistle better than the current theory. This proposed theory, which rests on the discussion in Lütgert's book and can be briefly stated, seems to me to explain well the points where the current theory fails. That it leaves some of Paul's utterances unexplained is not to be denied. After stating it I shall try to make a more detailed application of it (which Lütgert does not offer) to the continuous text of the epistle.

V

The Theory of Lütgert as here Elaborated

The hypothetical construction, freshly elaborated on the general basis of Lütgert's investigation, on which the proposed interpretation of Galatians rests is as follows:

When the letter was written, the Galatian churches, founded by Paul, included, or were harboring, some energetic persons (of gentile origin) who insisted that the observance of the Jewish Law was necessary to salvation, even for gentiles who believed in Christ. Their effort in this direction had led to a violent controversy (Gal. 5, 15; 5, 26; 6, 1) in which they were opposed by a party of 'pneumatici,' or what may be described as spiritualistic radicals. Paul had taught that faith in Christ is freely open to uncircumcised gentiles, and brings them the hope of salvation without their becoming subject in any manner to the Jewish Law; he had further taught that the gift of the Holy Spirit which God supplies causes believers to be in Christ a new creation, transforming them so that they are in the Spirit and not in the flesh, and live to God, the flesh with its passions and lusts being dead. Those who opposed the judaizers had fully accepted this teaching, but some of them, following Paul's clearly enunciated principle that those who are led by the Spirit are not under the Law but are free, allowed their freedom to be an occasion to the flesh, doubtless acting on a 'perfectionist' idea of the negligibility of moral discipline; such 'radicals' (as we may call them for convenience in the lack of a better term), priding themselves on their full reliance on the Spirit, were more distinguished by arrogance toward their brethren than by highly developed graces of character. In particular they were not altogether well disposed toward those in the local church who taught the word (6, 6). It must further be assumed that they definitely turned away (as, indeed, we might have expected) from Paul's emphasis on the fundamental relation of Christian faith to the Hebrew tradition and to the moral duties inculcated by the Law, an emphasis of which not only the Galatian epistle but also that to the Romans gives abundant illustration.[9] In a word, they were inclined to a doctrine akin to the teaching of Marcion a century later, and they strongly resemble the opponents who called out Paul's invective in 2 Corinthians, and who were, as it would seem to me, at the bottom of many of the difficulties dealt with in 1 Corinthians.

In the controversy in the Galatian churches it would be but natural (and it should be repeated that this whole picture, like that of the current theory, is only an hypothesis, designed to fit the facts of the epistle) that the judaizers should have emphasized the Hebraic elements which we know to have been prominent in Paul's system; the precise form of the bridge which they threw from these to their own demand for subjection to the Jewish Law it would be possible, but nor very profitable, to conjecture. That the judaizers attacked Paul, or declared him to be no regular apostle, need not be assumed; rather we may suppose that they distorted his teaching by illegitimate use of one element of it. On the opposing side, the radicals, who likewise exaggerated one element in Paul's teaching, were led to take a position of direct, and indeed bitter, hostility to him and to his leadership of gentile Christianity. They disparaged him personally, and declared that he had from the outset held but a subordinate position as an apostle, subject to the authority and the personal influence of the Jewish apostles in Jerusalem, to whom the radicals themselves felt no allegiance. In Paul's teaching, they said, he had weakly adapted himself to the ideas and preferences of his immediate environment; he had changed his gospel from the sound principles of freedom and new life in the Spirit which they themselves had adopted from him, and he had as good as preached circumcision itself. Some justification for this last thrust we might easily suppose to have been given by contentions of the judaizers as to the logical implications of certain of Paul's ideas, but it touched Paul, with his doctrine so carefully balanced and yet never swerving on that issue, in a peculiarly sensitive spot.

[9] This aspect of Romans is explained and emphasized in my paper, 'The Epistle to the Romans and Jewish Christianity,' in Studies in Early Christianity, edited by S. J. Case, presented to Frank Chamberlin Porter and Benjamin Wisner Bacon, New York, 1928.

If the judaizers claimed Paul's authority, they were nevertheless in reality farther removed from his principles than their opponents; on the other hand the radicals, with whom at bottom Paul stood nearer to agreement, became his enemies and disowned him altogether. Between these two, we should suppose, there must have been a body of Christians who loyally followed Paul in his via media, and tried to do justice to the various interests included in his comprehensive system. To them the teachers of the word (6, 6) may have belonged, and Paul's words (5, 9–10), "A little leaven leaveneth the whole lump: I have confidence in the Lord that ye will be none otherwise minded," suggests that he could count on a larger number of loyal adherents in these churches than the heated defence and sharp polemic of the epistle might otherwise lead us to suppose.

In this sketch the circumstances of the case have been imaginatively reconstructed in order to show that the resulting situation is conceivable. The only assumption, however, that is really essential for the theory under consideration is that there was a sharp conflict in Galatia between two extreme parties, each of which exaggerated one side of Paul's teaching, and that the chief bitterness against Paul was on the part of some of those who insisted, as he declares that he too does, on the independence of Christian faith from the Jewish Law and on the sufficiency of the Spirit.

VI

A Brief Commentary on the Epistle

The theory of the situation in Galatia which has just been outlined must now be put to the test by a brief commentary on the whole epistle, in which the theory will be followed, and such difficulties as attach to the theory will be manifest without special discussion. The term 'radicals' will be used to denote the party of 'pneumatici' who are assumed as opposing both the judaizers and Paul.

i . 1 The epistle is addressed, not to an erring or recalcitrant faction, but "to the churches of Galatia," as a whole. Perhaps the emphasis in the opening verse on the writer's divine commission as an apostle need not imply that that had been expressly denied; it may only mean that some brethren in the churches addressed have unbecomingly uttered themselves as if they denied it. These might be of either party, or of both, but in verses 11 and 12,

> For I make known to you, brethren, the gospel preached by me, that it is not according to man; for not from a man did I receive it, nor was I taught it, but through Jesus Christ's revelation,

the language and thought with reference to Paul's gospel closely resemble verse 1,

> Paul, Apostle, not from men, nor through a man, but through Jesus Christ and God the Father, who raised him from the dead.

It is therefore probable that the persons for whose benefit the autobiographical section (1, 13—2, 14) is to be introduced were already, though perhaps not exclusively, in mind in writing the impressive opening words of the epistle, and, as we shall see, the section 1, 13—2, 14 is directed against the radicals. In chapters 1 and 2, although a few verses are best taken as referring to the judaizers, it is remarkable that nothing is said which would lead us with certainty to assume their activity, or even their existence, if our insight were not later sharpened by 3, 1–6 and subsequent passages.

In the paragraph of the epistle containing the address Paul i. 2-5 takes occasion (vs. 4), as he does in Rom. 1, 2-4, to make a brief statement of the substance of his gospel, to the effect that, in accordance with the purpose of God, our Lord Jesus Christ died for our sins that he might rescue us from the present evil age. This statement would have been accepted as a principle by both parties, but the emphasis upon it here may be meant to intimate that in practice the judaizers (by which term I shall designate not only the propagandist leaders but the whole party which inclined toward circumcision and Jewish rites) were disposed to treat this divine provision for human salvation as inadequate. The significance, as explained below, of 2, 21,

For if salvation can be gained through the Law, then Christ died for naught,

confirms this view of the bearing and motive of 1, 4.

In an epistle of Paul (as in any other piece of writing) the i. 6-9 student must beware of treating the opening of a discussion as if it gave the key to the purpose of the whole. The writer's aim in any section, or in the whole, must be gauged by the conclusion into which his argument or exposition flows. That is the place where his purpose will commonly be made plain, and the reader must not permit his exegetical judgment to be guided by the mode which the writer happens to select — sometimes not quite wisely — for making a beginning. It is much as in the study of geography. The nature and course of a river are determined not by the swamps in which it rises and the rivulets in which it takes form near its source, but by its mouth, from which in historical fact it has gradually reached back to what are often the vague gropings of its sources on a crooked line of water-shed.

This may serve as a warning not to suppose that the interpretation of Galatians, chaps. 1 and 2, can be discovered from the abrupt and scornful outburst of 1, 6-9:

I am amazed that you are so quickly removing from him that called you in the grace of Christ unto another (ἕτερον) gospel, which is not other (ἄλλο), only there are some that trouble you (οἱ ταράσσοντες ὑμᾶς) and wish to pervert the gospel of Christ. But even if we, or an angel from heaven, preach the gospel to you in departure from what we preached to you, let him be anathema. As we have said before, now again I say, if anyone is preaching the gospel to you in departure from what you received, let him be anathema.

The amount of what Paul says here is: 'There can be but one gospel; you have allowed seditious and designing persons to induce you to pretend to alter it.' The emphasis on "the grace of Christ," as well as all the language used, support the view that Paul is here reproving the judaizing element, by reason of whose attitude and tendency, indeed, the whole trouble has broken out, and which under any theory (see 5, 9–10; 6, 12; 6, 16) is not to be understood as constituting the whole membership of these churches. But the interpretation thus put on these verses (6–9) should not be allowed to control the understanding of what follows.

i. 10 The apostle's choice of this path of approach to his subject, if the usual interpretation is right (as it probably is), sets him here at the outset squarely in opposition to the whole judaizing movement. He gives the most solemn assurance that in nothing does his present preaching depart from that which he has presented to the Galatians in his former visits to them. That is substantially all he says in verses 8–9. They seem to proceed from the same motive as the compact statement of his gospel in verse 4, and serve effectively to dissociate him from the judaizers. The two passages taken together are a sharp reproof of the judaizers, but they also serve to establish the position from which he next proceeds, as I conceive, to make his defence against the radicals.

'One,' he says in verse 10, 'who can speak as I have just spoken can fairly claim to have demonstrated his sincerity and independence.' His words are:

> For am I now striving for the favor of men or of God (ἀνθρώπους πείθω ἢ τὸν θεόν)? or am I seeking to please men? If I were still pleasing men, I should not be Christ's servant.

What Paul means by this is to be understood from the weighty passage that follows, running as far at least as 2, 14. And here the theory we are following breaks completely with the usual explanation. A color for the charge of insincerity and dependence on men for his gospel was in fact provided by the prominence which Paul's teaching gave to the Hebrew tradition (see Rom. 3, 1–2; 3, 21; Rom. 4, etc.), and by the misuse which the

Galatian judaizers may well have made of that aspect of his real teaching. It is not against the judaizers that his affirmation of his independence is directed; on the contrary his defence is against a reproach from the side of the radicals, who are saying that he is insincere and pliable, and that the Jewish taint which his gospel originally received from the Jerusalem apostles has now led him to compromise with the principles he had formerly affirmed.

In this passage, from 1, 11 to 2, 14, the outline of the argu- i. 11–ii. 14 ment is at most points easily traced, but in some sentences the emphasis, which is essential to the interpretation, is doubtful. The fuller discussion in the early part of this essay attempted to bring into relief the infelicities of the current theory, when applied to these verses. Let us see, by means of a paraphrase and abridgment, what our alternative theory can do.

'My gospel,' says Paul, 'was not taught me by men, but was revealed to me by God, whose definite purpose in creating me was that I should preach the gospel among the gentiles. On my conversion I kept away from the leaders of the church for three years, and then, when I did visit Jerusalem, I stayed with Peter for only two weeks, and of the other apostles saw no one (before God, this is the truth!) except James the Lord's brother. Thereafter I was in Syria and Cilicia, and the churches of Judaea saw nothing of me; their friendly attitude was due solely to hearsay reports of my preaching in gentile lands. Then, after fourteen years, I admit that I went up to Jerusalem again with Barnabas and Titus (an uncircumcised gentile), but I went because God expressly directed me so to do. On that occasion, I grant, I did set forth to the leading men my gospel, and did so in a private interview, lest through any misunderstanding of it my work among the gentiles should be interfered with and prove to have been in vain. But it was not made necessary even that Titus should be circumcised, although there were present false brethren with malicious purpose directed against gentile freedom and the truth of the gospel, to whom I yielded subjection not for a single moment.[10] The result was that (quite the con-

---

[10] It is not here incumbent on us to disentangle the difficult syntax of this passage. But it may be said that in verse 5, although the reading without the nega-

trary of the way in which the matter has been misrepresented in Galatia) the leaders at Jerusalem, James, Cephas, and John (of whose supposed authority I make nothing at all), had to admit that I have been entrusted by God with the gospel of the gentiles; and they had to give full recognition to my and Barnabas' work. Later, when Cephas came to Antioch, I maintained my independence and entirely refused to admit that his withdrawal from the common meals of the church was justified, although in this instance Barnabas sided with him.'

In the passage, as every theory must recognize, Paul is substantiating from the facts of his life the affirmation of his independence and consistency. In framing my paraphrase I have tried to bring out what seems to me the bearing of his argument, and have not, I trust, done any violence to the meaning of his language. In explaining so fully the exact nature of the result of the conference at Jerusalem (2, 4–10) his motive seems to be the need of showing, in self-defence, that no influence was then exerted on him which was capable of affecting his gospel; when he states that the Jerusalem apostles had been compelled to give full recognition to the gospel of freedom as he preached it, that fact is not affirmed with pride, but rather explained, almost apologized for, as harmless. If he had used a clearer word than προσανέθεντο (vs. 6) to state what the apostles did not do, our understanding would be easier, but in any case, whatever the term he uses may exactly mean, he seems by it to designate what his enemies had incorrectly alleged to have taken place. The whole passage (1, 11—2, 14) suits well the idea of a defence against the misrepresentations of the radicals; the great difficulties of the usual theory, by which the passage has to be interpreted as a reply to charges brought by the judaizers, have already been sufficiently urged. Under the proposed theory these difficulties completely disappear.

---

tive (οὐδέ) is unquestionably old, neither that reading nor the corresponding interpretation of the ordinary text (namely, that Titus was indeed circumcised, but as a voluntary act and not under compulsion) can possibly be accepted, since either would involve the admission by Paul that he yielded 'by subjection.' That is impossible in this context. Paul might have admitted that he 'yielded,' but never that his yielding was a 'subjection'!

Exactly where the rebuke to Peter which begins in 2, 14 ends, ii. 15-21
it is not important to determine. In any case Paul moves
rapidly into a positive statement of his own theological position,
and his statement (2, 15–21) suits our theory admirably.

'We Jews,' he says, 'who have believed in Christ, rely for
salvation on faith; by the works of the Law no man will be
justified. But if, while relying on Christ, we nevertheless still
commit sin [as Paul, in contradiction of the perfectionism of the
radicals, is compelled by the facts to admit that we do], that
does not imply the absurdity that it is Christ who causes us
to sin, so as to make my position [namely, that believers must
pay attention to morals] untenable. By faith in Christ I have
broken the power of sin; if I thereafter yield to that power, it
is I who make myself a transgressor; the fault is my own [and
no defect is to be ascribed to Christ or to the transforming
power of faith in Him]. I am wholly severed from the Law,
and have new life unto God. I am crucified with Christ, and
my life is not mine but His. I continue, indeed, to live in the
flesh, but none the less my life is lived in faith in the Son of God
who died to save me. It is false to say that [because I hold a
believer to be capable of sin] I treat the grace of God as worth-
less. Salvation (δικαιοσύνη)[11] is not gained through the Law; to
affirm that it is so gained would indeed be equivalent to denying
the need and efficacy of the saving death of Christ. No one
shall say that of me!'

The interpretation of this passage is at many points disputable, but the explanation offered in my paraphrase seems to be
consonant with the language, especially at all the critical points,
and it certainly makes sense, provided the theory of the whole
epistle which we are following is accepted. The key to the purpose and meaning of Paul's flaming and vehement words must
be looked for in verses 20 and 21: 'My doctrine is not open to
the objection that it makes Christ's death superfluous.' He is

[11] For the reasons for holding that 'salvation' is the proper meaning of δικαιοσύνη in such a passage as this I would refer to my article ' "Righteousness" and
"The Righteousness of God" in the Old Testament and in St. Paul' in the Journal
of Biblical Literature, XXII, 1903, pp. 211–227. See also G. F. Moore, Judaism,
1927, II, pp. 171–172.

clearly on the defensive here, and the whole of verses 17–21 becomes comprehensible so soon as they are taken as repelling the charge that Paul's view, if consistently developed, would make Christ a minister of sin, make void the grace of God, imply that salvation is by the Law, and lead to the blasphemous absurdity that Christ died with no adequate result. Such charges as these can have come only from the radicals; they had affirmed, it would seem, that by not carrying his principles through to their logical perfectionist conclusion, and by allowing, as we know he did, at least a qualified significance to much that is contained in the Law, Paul completely emasculated his original gospel. All this Paul indignantly denies; and he passionately affirms the completeness of his break with the Law, the unqualified newness of his life in Christ, and his sole reliance for salvation on the grace offered through Christ's death on the cross. As we shall see later, it is on precisely this same ground that he rests in his offensive against the radicals in 5, 11—6, 10.

iii. 1   This superb conclusion of the sceond chapter well prepares for the transition of 3, 1:

> O foolish Galatians, who has bewitched you, before whose eyes Jesus Christ was openly set forth crucified?

Paul has now established his position as against the radicals' charge that under the influence of the Jerusalem apostles he has receded from the principles of the gospel he once preached. What he has written ought to be enough to show the radicals that his conduct is not open to the objections they have made, and that his doctrine is not untrue to his principles, which are the same as their own. He can now turn again to the judaizers, to whom he had addressed his opening remonstrance in 1, 6–7, and by whose wretched proposals the quarrel was raised which brought out the radicals' hostility to himself. But also, by what he proceeds to say, he gives still further engagement to the radicals that his closing sentence in 2, 21, "if salvation (δικαιοσύνη) comes through the Law, then Christ died for naught," is sincere, and that he is ready to act on the principle there affirmed. It is to be noted that the emotional tone shows no break between chapters 2 and 3, but there is a close emotional kinship between 1, 6 and 3, 1–5, and the whole section, 1, 10 to 2, 21, is now seen to be of the nature of a digression from the main line of direct attack upon which he entered at 1, 6. This circumstance is overlooked in the customary treatment of the epistle as consisting of three successive, coördinate sections of two chapters each: (1) Personal, (2) Doctrinal, or Refutatory, (3) Hortatory. The disposition which I would follow is analogous, rather, to that of Romans, chapters 1–3, where Rom. 1, 18—3, 20 is likewise a long and impressive digression, after which Paul returns to his main line of thought with an echo of the very language of Romans 1, 17.

The argument of Galatians 3,2–5, is perfectly adapted to its purpose, and requires no special comment: iii. 2–5

> This only would I learn from you, Was it in consequence of (ἐξ) the works of the Law or of the hearing (or message) of faith that you received the Spirit? Are you so foolish? Having begun by the Spirit do you now finish by the flesh? Have you suffered so many things in vain? if it be indeed in vain. He therefore who supplies to you the Spirit and who works miracles among you, [does he do it] in consequence of (ἐξ) the works of the Law or of the hearing (or message) of faith?

In passing, it is worth while to note that the possession of the Spirit, which our theory takes to have been a watchword of the radicals, is here assumed to be the test of God's manifest favor in the eyes of the whole church, and that Paul (3, 3) expressly refers to the inferiority of the things of the flesh to those of the Spirit.

What follows (3, 6—4, 7), as I have urged above, is not satis- iii. 6–iv. 7 factorily explained by the current theory that the whole epistle is governed by the argument with the judaizers. The fact is rather that in the passage beginning with 3, 6 Paul goes on to explain exactly what his own position is, inclusive of both its complementary aspects. That his doctrine has in fact two aspects, one of them decidedly Jewish in character, is the reason why the radicals attack him, and it is necessary for him somewhere to show as convincingly as he can, not only that he is opposed to the adoption of the Law by gentiles, but also that there is no inconsistency between this opposition and the value he ascribes to the Hebrew tradition. That is what he is really doing in the section before us, although at the same time the passage is an attack on judaizing tendencies, with an argument against those who promote them. Only by this supposition can we account for the singular balanced qualification of his arguments in 3, 6—4, 7, as contrasted with the downright positiveness of 3, 2–5. The Law, he says, is totally ineffective to bring salvation, and faith in Christ frees believers from any relation to the Law. But he has in mind all through, and keeps pointing out, that this Christian faith brings gentiles, though uncircumcised, into direct relation, if not to the Law, yet to the Hebrew tradition and the promises of God made to Abraham; all believers, whether Jews or gentiles, are true heirs, and indeed the only true heirs, of the covenant with Abraham. As to the Law itself, his teaching is clear-cut. The death of Christ has brought it about that believers, gentiles as well as Jews, receive the blessing of Abraham and the gift of the Spirit — and the two are identical (3, 14 puts the two parallel in a way that sharply hits the radicals); the Law is of no value for salvation. And yet the Law is not contrary to the promises of God; it was given by God (although at the hand of a mediator). But it was temporary and has now come to its predestined and intended termination. It had its own function; that has now been discharged, and faith has come.

All this balanced elaboration of his precise position (which in parts strongly reminds the reader of Romans 7) has but qualified usefulness for Paul's attack on judaizing tendencies, but is of great importance for explaining to the radicals how, without abandoning his doctrine of freedom, he can yet have so much to say about Abraham and the Jewish relationships of Christianity. In fact, the idea of Christianity as a distinct religion, as we often conceive it, would have shocked Paul.[12] The line of God's saving work was continuous, and from the beginning until the death of Christ that line came down without interruption through Hebrew history. When the fulness of

---

[12] Hort observes: "The last thing that St Paul would ever have thought of saying of the Gospel was that it was a new religion. In his eyes, as with all the Apostles, it was the old religion of Israel carried to perfection, not a new faith superseding it" (Prolegomena to St Paul's Epistles to the Romans and the Ephesians, p. 25).

time came, God sent his Son to earth as a Jew (4, 5), and re-
demption, with the gift of the Spirit of the Son of God, has
thereby been brought to believers, among whom there is no
distinction between Jews and gentiles any more than between
bond and free or male and female.

Paul's careful statement of both sides of his doctrine does
not add to its force as an attack on judaizing sentiment; but
he throws his argument into this form because he is thus able
to demonstrate that he is not recreant to his avowed principle
of freedom, and is by no means open to the charge of "preaching
circumcision." He gains his point by making clear what is the
real ground, and what are the limits, of that respect on his part
for the Hebrew tradition and the Law which has caused the
radicals to misrepresent and attack him. In fundamental principle, as distinguished from doctrinaire application, he sets
himself squarely against the judaizers and in verses 4–7 (which
close the little section) he states his position with perfect pre-
cision and compactness for the benefit of both the parties that
he is opposing: 'It is through a Jew, who was the Son of God,
that we receive adoption as God's sons; but to sons is given
the Spirit of God's Son, and the freedom and heritage of sons'
(compare Rom. 1, 2–4). There is no comfort here for the judaizers, but at the same time Paul insists on an aspect of truth
which the radicals (who boast that they "live by the Spirit")
are prone to forget.

On the foundation laid in 4, 1–7, where the period before iv. 8–11
Christ is compared to the minority of an heir, and enslavement
to the 'rudiments of the world' contrasted with freedom in
the possession of the Spirit, rests the passage 4, 8–11:

> But at that time, not knowing God, you became enslaved to them that by
> nature are no gods; but now, having come to know God, or rather to be known
> by God, how is it that you return again to the weak and poverty-stricken
> rudiments, to which over again you desire to become enslaved? You are
> observing days and months and seasons and years. I fear with regard to you
> (φοβοῦμαι ὑμᾶς) lest I have labored for you (εἰς ὑμᾶς) in vain.

Before the death of Christ, an event decisive in the history of
the human race, men were enslaved under the rudiments of the
world (if that is what the difficult word στοχεῖα means in this

Galatian context), and Paul evidently means the statement to apply both to Jews and to gentiles. (This both on general principles and because 'we' in 4, 3 can hardly refer to Jews alone, since that interpretation would result in making the gentiles of the period before Christ superior in their freedom to the Jews.) The gentiles were in fact enslaved to false gods (vs. 8). Christ has set them free, and Paul appeals to them (vss. 9–11) not to return again to the rudiments, as, by the observance of Jewish days and seasons, they are beginning to do. Perhaps the contemptuous reference to these days and seasons, in a passage where the servitude of the Jewish Law and that of heathen worship are set parallel, has in view the unexpressed thought, 'just as the heathen do.' That supposition would explain, what is otherwise somewhat difficult to understand, why Paul here mentions only these judaizing practices, and not, as elsewhere (for instance in 5, 2–4), circumcision.

iv. 12–20   The continuation of the appeal in 4, 12–20 alludes to circumstances of which otherwise we know nothing, and in consequence contains abundant obscurities. In view of what precedes, and of what follows in the allegory of 4,21 ff., it is necessary to take the whole paragraph as part of Paul's appeal to the soberminded among the Galatians not to be led astray by the judaizing element. The theory we are pursuing does not seem to contribute to the explanation of this passage, in spite of Lütgert's attempt to throw new light on it.

iv. 21–v. 10   Of the allegory, 4, 21–31, enough has been said above. Paul still lingers over the relation to Abraham, and after his drastic application of the Old Testament in verse 30,

But what saith the Scripture? "Cast out the handmaid and her son, for the son of the handmaid shall not inherit with the son of the freewoman,"

he passes to a concluding summary (5, 1–10) for this central section of the epistle, which began with chapter 3, and which has as its ostensible main purpose the refutation and rebuke of the judaizers.

v. 11–12   The transition to the next topic is an important one, sharper than any other transition in the epistle. Our theory requires the break to be made after verse 10, not after verse 12. The reproof to the judaizers has been concluded, and likewise Paul's defence against the radicals substantially achieved. It remained to touch, with severity and for us very instructively, on what was in Paul's eyes the most objectionable aspect of the radicals' teaching and influence, namely, their perfectionist disregard of moral discipline. To his apprehension this was doubtless associated with their complete severance of Christianity from the Hebrew tradition, and was a subject to which, as we have seen, he has probably made reference already in 2, 17–21.

Now, however, before entering upon this matter, he again breaks out, in a manner not unlike his change of the object of his animadversion in 1, 10, and with a sudden, and brief, burst of indignation, into a violent repudiation of the radicals' worst misrepresentation of him. Verses 11 and 12 do not in our interpretation bear any relation to what immediately precedes them; with what follows they are connected by a conjunction ('for,' vs. 13). This connection is appropriate, since, although the grounds of his complaint in vss. 11–12 and in 5, 13—6, 10 are distinct, the persons who give cause for it are the same. Verses 11–12 read thus:

> But I, brethren, if I am still preaching circumcision, why am I still persecuted? In that case the stumblingblock of the cross has been done away. Would that those who are unsettling you would even mutilate themselves (ὄφελον καὶ ἀποκόψονται οἱ ἀναστατοῦντες ὑμᾶς)!

The thought underlying these words may be expanded by such a paraphrase as this:

> Look at me [he cries]; does anyone say that I still preach circumcision, as before my conversion; that I am still a Jew at heart and not, first of all and throughout my whole being, a believer, crucified with Christ, dead to the law, in whom Christ — not myself — lives? The persecution I endure for Christ refutes the notion. For one who preaches circumcision the cross of Christ is no source of personal risk. Those who are trying to lay you waste — I only wish they would ruin themselves!

The precise meaning of the last sentence is doubtful,[13] but its general sense and the fierce vigor of the emotion that called it

[13] It is difficult to find oneself at ease with Lütgert's explanation of this sentence, although he is right in deeming it part of Paul's attack on the radicals. He thinks (pp. 31–34) that Paul regards the practices of his radical opponents as the intrusion of heathen religious frenzy into the life of Christian churches in

forth are unmistakable. Its context and position show that it
refers to the radicals, not to the judaizers. To produce the
desired effect, however, Paul must restrain his speech, and
although the seriousness of the evils reproved in what follows
reveals to us the cause of the outburst, the language takes a
quieter tone.

Paul's stinging rebuke to these personal charges against himself is due not only to natural human resentment, but also to
the fact that the outrage proceeds from the same detestable
attitude which has misused liberty for the false ends of license,
and which, while pluming itself on its superiority in the Spirit
has in fact given an occasion to the flesh. A masterly passage
follows, nearly every sentence of which gains in interest and
force from the concrete application which our theory of the
general situation enables us to make. Indeed, as De Wette saw
and others have more dimly felt, this passage calls imperatively
for the explanation which Lütgert's theory supplies.

v. 13–17   Verse 13,

> For to freedom have you been called, brethren, only [use] not your freedom
> so that it becomes (εἰς) an occasion to the flesh, but through love serve one
> another,

opens with 'for,' and the conjunction belongs not to the first
clause but to the second ('[use] not your freedom'). The in-
dignant tone of verses 11 and 12 is explained by the danger
against which verse 13 brings its warning, the danger namely
that the freedom which the radicals rightly claim will lead to
sin. Security in this direction can be gained only by a domi-
nant purpose of mutual service in love, the very oppposite to
the present actual situation of acute conflict in the churches

---

Galatia, and that Paul means to say, 'I wish that the heathenism of this whole
business might be brought into full daylight, and that the leaders would openly
declare themselves as heathen by adopting the horrible custom of the priests of
Cybele, the circle to which they really belong.' This seems forced, though I have
no adequate alternative to offer. In any case it is impossible to believe that Paul
was capable of making so offensive a comparison of the rite of circumcision with
castration as the usual theory finds it necessary to assume. Phil. 3, 2 does not
justify such a view, for κατατομή merely refers to ritual cuttings, for instance of
the hands; to the examples of the verb given by Lightfoot, ad loc., add (for the
noun) Jer. 48, 37 in the version of Symmachus.

(vss. 14–15). If these self-conscious claimants to the possession of the Spirit will only in practice walk by the Spirit, they will then be victorious over the demand of the flesh for indulgence (vs. 16); for as a matter of fact life in the Spirit is not such plain sailing as these perfectionists pretend, the flesh is an active enemy, you find yourself failing to carry out what your will directs (vs. 17). The whole passage (vss. 14–17) runs as follows:

> For the whole Law is fulfilled in one precept, namely, "Thou shalt love thy neighbor as thyself"; but if you bite and devour one another, take heed that you be not consumed by one another.
> But I say, walk by the Spirit and you will not fulfil the desire of the flesh. For the desire of the flesh is contrary to that of the Spirit (ἡ γὰρ σὰρξ ἐπιθυμεῖ κατὰ τοῦ πνεύματος) and that of the Spirit contrary to that of the flesh, for these [Spirit and flesh] are opposed to one another, that you may not do what you wish.

Paul goes on (again I paraphrase): 'I am entirely at one with you in your claim that if you are in the Spirit, you are not under the Law. But it is the flesh, not the Spirit, which produces the well-known vices against which I still have to warn you now as I have done before. The fruit the Spirit bears consists of love, joy, peace, and the other recognized virtues. So far as concerns conduct and character, the Spirit works toward precisely the same end at which the Law (understood as summed up in the one commandment of Love) aims. You cannot neglect these virtues on the ground that it is merely the Law that inculcates them. If you belong, as you claim, to Christ Jesus, you must by your own self-discipline check the passions which the flesh kindles, and follow with your own active will the type of character which the Spirit fosters. If our life is in the Spirit, let our walk and conversation be there too' (vss. 18–26). v. 18–26

In what follows (6, 1–10) Paul applies this teaching in detail, and with complete calmness and moderation of expression. Upon those who possess the Spirit it is incumbent to practice gentleness toward those who do wrong ('you yourselves are not raised above the possibility of being tempted'), and helpfulness, and renunciation of all arrogance. These persons ought to make their fair contribution to the support of the teachers of the word. God cannot be deceived; he looks with displeasure vi. 1–10 on the works of the flesh, whoever they come from. We must not relax our endeavor. The present time will come to an end; and the space before that end arrives is our only opportunity to do our duty to the world and to our brethren.

The whole force of this passage (5, 13—6, 10) seems to turn on the claim of the persons addressed that they are 'spiritual' and as such free from responsibility for their own conduct. It is implied that they are engaged in bitter controversy with their brethren, are inconsiderate, harsh, and arrogant, and have shown themselves unwilling to bear the common burden of the churches. Our picture of the radicals is largely dependent on the indications of these verses, and more than once they recall the traits declared in 2 Corinthians to be exhibited by the similar group of Paul's opponents in that place.

vi. 11-18 The conclusion of the epistle (6, 11–18) offers some problems of interpretation, but they need not be discussed here. It is natural that after the long section dealing solely with the radicals (5, 11—6, 10) a sharp word against the judaizers should recur, natural also that Paul should solemnly affirm that the sole ground of any right he may have to appeal for loyalty to himself is the Cross of Christ, whereby he has become detached from every worldly aim. When he says, "For neither is circumcision anything, nor uncircumcision, but a new creation" (6, 15) he repeats the formula, already twice given a place in this epistle (3, 28; 5, 6), which he feels to be the best expression of his positive position. If believers will walk by that principle, the blessing of God will follow them.

A pathetic, perhaps half-humorous, sigh, 'I wish I might be done with these troubles; I wear scars received in Jesus' service,' leads to the closing benediction.

VII

The Claims of the Proposed Theory; the Origin of the Judaizing Influence; the Date of the Epistle

The theory of Lütgert, as I have attempted to develop it, is recommended by its applicability in varying ways to each of the four sections which make up substantially the whole epistle (1, 10—6, 10). First, it suits the hortatory section (5, 11—6, 10) perfectly, and in the past something of the sort has at that point more than once suggested itself to scholars, though they have but rarely accepted the suggestion. Secondly, for the autobiographical narrative (1, 10—2, 14) this theory gives an apt interpretation, naturally suggested by the passage, whereas the usual interpretation labors under serious difficulties. Thirdly, the fine verses of personal confession (2, 15–21) into which the narrative section almost imperceptibly merges, are made much easier to understand, both in themselves and in their position in the epistle and their relation to the thought of the whole. Fourthly, in the anti-judaist division itself (3, 1—5, 10) much that is broadly developed but yet seems not quite to fit the requirements of Paul's argument, becomes perfectly appropriate so soon as we recognize that the apostle has in mind not only the judaizers but equally their radical opponents, and that for the benefit of the latter he expounds not one side only but the full circle of his doctrine concerning the Law and the Hebrew tradition. The few remaining verses of the epistle, at the opening and close, at least present no difficulties to the application of the theory. Further, the transitions of thought, which under the current theory have often been deemed abrupt, are severally more natural if the writer has in view two parties, in conflict with each other and both needing to be regulated, instead of only one. Especially helpful in this respect is the observation that the whole passage, 1, 10—2, 21, is of the nature of a digression, after which the argument of 3, 1 returns to the thought of 1, 9.

These are the substantial grounds on which a claim is made for the theory. Many single passages in the epistle will always remain without convincing explanation because they allude in general terms to matters of which we, unlike the original readers, are totally ignorant, but none of these passages seems to forbid our theory. One of them is 1, 18–19, with its singular emphasis on two weeks' intercourse with only Cephas and James, as if that disproved the personal influence on Paul which his detractors alleged. The question arises whether Cephas and James were considered harmless, while some third member, or group of members, of the Jerusalem apostolate was really in mind. Lütgert thinks of John, but the suggestion is difficult to accept. This question, however, arises under any view of the bearing of Paul's general argument, and the uncertainty in no way detracts from the strength of our theory.

A question of some importance is that of the origin of the judaizing influences. It is clearly implied (1, 7; 4, 17; 5, 10; 6, 12–13) that certain individual leaders, probably not very numerous (5, 9), are to blame for instigating the movement, and (6, 12) that these persons were Christian believers, not unbelieving Jews, nor of course unbelieving heathen. It is commonly assumed that these disturbers came into the Galatian communities from outside, but nothing in the epistle positively indicates this, and the absence of evidence to the contrary does not constitute a valid argument for the assumption. Many writers on the epistle go farther, and, without any evidence at all, affirm, sometimes with great positiveness, that the disturbance in Galatia was due to Palestinian Jewish believers in Christ who came from Jerusalem expressly as emissaries to try to break up Paul's work. The affair is understood as a further extension of what is supposed to have been attempted at Antioch (Gal. 2, 12), and as part of an organized anti-pauline missionary enterprise. This unsupported hypothesis, for it is nothing more, has entered deeply into the prevalent general picture of the Apostolic Age, or at least of its earlier years.

But another hypothesis is equally possible and has the advantage of not requiring the assumption of a whole series of unattested facts otherwise unknown to us. In the Christian church from an early time Jewish ceremonies and customs had a strong attraction for certain classes, and their appeal continued for centuries to disturb the mind of Christian pastors. Ignatius (*Magnesians* 8–10, *Philadelphians* 6–8) was concerned about this tendency at Antioch in his time, and the persistence of the attraction is shown in the same city as much as three centuries later by Chrysostom's attacks on the habit that many Christians then had of taking part in the rites of the Jews, especially the day of atonement. Against it he delivered eight *Orationes adversus Judaeos*, and in his exegetical homilies on Galatians (Homily 1, on Gal. 1, 7) he actually uses these objectionable habits of Antiochian Christians of his own day to illustrate at some length what Paul meant in Galatians. "There are many of us now," he says, "who fast on the same day as the Jews and keep the sabbaths in the same manner"— and the distance in time makes the parallel all the more impressive. Such an influence as this, working in the Galatian churches in Paul's time, is entirely comprehensible, and would account for the judaizing movement without any supposition of emissaries from Palestine. Indeed no Christians of Jewish birth in Galatia are definitely indicated by Paul, and none need be thought of as playing any part in the controversy which gave rise to the epistle. All that we need suppose is that certain gentile Christians had proved susceptible to the efforts of local synagogue Jews, and had tried to persuade the churches as a whole to accept Jewish rites, including circumcision. Such a knot of judaizing gentile Christians, in one or more of the churches would seem to satisfy Paul's references to disturbers of the peace. He attributes (6, 12–13) to these judaistically inclined gentiles a motive of cowardice in the face of a persecution which apparently proceeded from the side of the Jews (4, 29; 5, 11), and a contemptible desire to increase their own prestige (4, 17; 6, 12–13) — charges as to the justice of which we can form no opinion. Under the hypothesis here suggested the ultimate origin of the judaizing influences had nothing to do with Jerusalem.[14]

[14] In the ordinary theory the difficulty is generally overlooked that a missionary enterprise at such a distance would in itself have been hard to handle, and especially hard for Christians so poor that Paul had to collect money for their relief.

On the moot question of the date of the Epistle to the Galatians the general theory here presented throws no direct light. But since the theory wholly detaches the controversy in Galatia from the Jerusalem controversy of Acts 15, it becomes easier to assign the epistle to a relatively late moment in the period of Paul's free missionary activity. The controversy with the Galatian radicals recalls 2 Corinthians, and was far more ominous for the future than the controversy with the judaizers. To the Epistle to the Romans the Galatian epistle itself shows manifold similarity, not only in individual turns of phrase and mode of thought but in the whole balanced theological teaching whereby freedom from the Law and respect for the Hebrew tradition are affirmed with equal insistence. Nevertheless the emotional frame of the writer is different in Romans, and the mood in Galatians is far more like that of 2 Corinthians. There seems no longer any sufficient reason for assigning the epistle to a very early date — before the arrival at Ephesus (Acts 19, 1) — unless it be the words "so quickly" of Gal. 1, 6; and the force of these words is diminished by the implication usually found in Gal. 4, 13 that Paul had already visited these churches more than once. At any rate he is far enough away at the moment of writing to have no thought of coming to settle their difficulties in person (4, 20).

This theory of the situation in the Galatian churches, presented by Lütgert and here freshly worked out, seems to explain the Epistle to the Galatians better than has hitherto been possible, and itself not to be exposed to serious objection from the implications of the epistle. At the same time it brings the epistle more fully into the general stream of interest of the period when it was written. On our conception of Paul's ideas and purposes, and on our general picture of the Apostolic Age, it is not without its bearing.

Harvard Theological Studies

In press

THE OLD GEORGIAN VERSION OF ST. EPIPHANIUS ON THE TWELVE PRECIOUS STONES, with a Translation and Introduction. By Robert P. Blake, Associate Professor of History in Harvard University.